A GUIDE TO ROSH HA-SHANAH

By the same author
WE HAVE REASON TO BELIEVE
JEWISH PRAYER
A GUIDE TO YOM KIPPUR

A GUIDE TO
ROSH HA-SHANAH

by
RABBI LOUIS JACOBS, B.A., Ph.D.
Minister, New West End Synagogue
London

JEWISH CHRONICLE PUBLICATIONS
London

Published by
JEWISH CHRONICLE PUBLICATIONS
37 *Furnival Street, London, EC4*
© Louis Jacobs, 1959

For my MOTHER-IN-LAW
and in memory of my
FATHER-IN-LAW

Made and printed in Great Britain by
THE SHARON PRESS
31 *Furnival Street, London, EC4*

CONTENTS

CHAPTER I

ROSH HA-SHANAH

Introduction

Joy AND sadness are twins and the closeness of their relationship is never seen more clearly than at the new year. The old year with its disappointments and frustrations has departed, the new year with its promise of fulfilment has dawned. It is natural for thoughtful people to call a halt to the busy tempo of their lives and use the new year season for reflection on life's problems, its meaning and its purpose. This is why the Jewish new year festival is not an occasion for indulging in hilarity or exuberant mirth but the beginning of the ten days of penitence when men are called upon to reassess the value of their lives and consider how the quality can be improved. But for all his dissatisfaction with his present course the man of faith affirms that life is God-given and worth living. *Rosh Ha-Shanah* is a solemn festival but it is a festival. The key-note of the day is a spirit of quiet confidence in which man seeks to overcome the hindrances to better living by placing his trust in God.

With *Yom Kippur*, the festival of *Rosh Ha-Shanah* has come to take pride of place in the Jewish calendar. The powerful fascination of those 'Days of Awe' continues to draw the majority of Jews into the Synagogue. Although present-day Jewish preachers tend to deplore this 'three times a year' Judaism—and so far as Judaism is a religion intended to embrace the whole of life their criticism is well-founded—yet it is in many ways an encouraging sign of the basic appeal of our faith that at least on these days its challenge does not go unheard. The man who is godly in his spare time is far removed from the Jewish ideal; constant persistence in the path of duty rather than periodic bouts of religiosity is Judaism's demand on its adherents. But it is not unusual for men and women to change the whole course of their lives under the influence of the lovely home ceremonies and stirring Synagogue services of the 'Days of Awe'. Here it is possible, in the expressive words of the Rabbis, for a man to 'acquire his eternity in one hour'.

In the Bible

THE Bible nowhere speaks of the festival we now call *Rosh Ha-Shanah* as the new year. The term *Rosh Ha-Shanah* is found in Scripture—'In the five and twentieth year of our captivity, *in the beginning of the year*, in the tenth day of the month, in the fourteenth year after the city was smitten, in the self-same day, the hand of the Lord was upon me, and He brought me thither' (*Ez.* xl:1) —but there is no reference here to the festival celebrated at this period. Following the beginning of the Exodus is the command (the first, the Rabbis note, to be addressed to all Israel) to count the months of the year from the Spring month, the month of deliverance from Egyptian bondage. Consequently, the month we now call by the Babylonian name *Tishri* is called, in the Bible, 'the seventh month', i.e. counting from the Spring month

2

we now call by the Babylonian name *Nisan*. During the Babylonian exile the Jews adopted some of the Babylonian forms including the names of the months, the names of the angels, and, according to some Rabbis, the script in which the Torah is now written. It is of interest that the Babylonian name *Tishri* appears to be derived from the root *seru*, which means 'to begin'. Possibly, in Babylon, too, this month was the beginning of the year. In the Bible we read that the first day of the seventh month was to be celebrated as a feast-day, no work was to be done unless it were for the preparation of food, and the trumpet was to be blown:

'And the Lord spoke unto Moses saying: Speak unto the children of Israel, saying: In the seventh month, in the first day of the month, shall be a solemn rest unto you, a memorial proclaimed with the blast of horns, a holy convocation. Ye shall do no manner of servile work; and ye shall bring an offering made by fire unto the Lord.' (*Lev.* xxiii: 23-25)

'And in the seventh month, on the first day of the month, ye shall have a holy convocation: ye shall do no manner of servile work; it is a day of blowing the horn unto you. And ye shall prepare a burnt-offering for a sweet savour unto the Lord: one young bullock, one ram, seven he-lambs of the first year without blemish; and their meal-offering, fine flour mingled with oil, three-tenth parts for the bullock, two-tenth parts for the ram, and one-tenth part for every lamb of the seven lambs; and one he-goat for a sin-offering, to make atonement for you; beside the burnt-offering of the new

3

moon, and the meal-offering thereof, and the continual
burnt-offering, and the meal offering thereof, and their
drink-offerings, according unto their ordinance, for a
sweet savour, an offering made by fire unto the Lord.'
(*Num.* xxix : 1-6)

What was the purpose of this festival? Which events
did it commemorate? Scripture is silent on these questions. But we do know that some ancient Semitic
peoples thought of the year as beginning in the autumn,
at the time of the late harvest. It is highly plausible,
therefore, to see the Biblical festival as a harvest feast,
marking the beginning of the agricultural year. In other
words, the Israelites had two ways of counting their
years, from the Spring month, in remembrance of the
Exodus, and from the seventh month, the natural, agricultural period of commencement. If this is correct, the
later Rabbinic name for the festival *Rosh Ha-Shanah*
(New Year) only makes explicit that which had been
implicit in its observance from the earliest times.

It was on the first day of the seventh month that Ezra,
the Scribe, the great leader who in the Rabbinic tradition
is second only to Moses as the teacher of the Torah, read
the book of the Torah before his people. This is how the
book of Nehemiah describes the dramatic occasion when
the Israelites, who had returned from the Babylonian
captivity to rebuild the land of their fathers, renewed
their covenant with God:

> *And Ezra the priest brought the Law before the con-*
> *gregation, both men and women, and all that could hear*
> *with understanding, upon the first day of the seventh*

*month. And he read therein before the broad place that
was before the water gate from early morning until mid-
day, in the presence of the men and the women, and of
those that could understand; and the ears of all the
people were attentive unto the book of the Law. . . .And
they read in the book, in the Law of God, distinctly; and
they gave the sense, and caused them to understand the
reading.* (*Neh.* viii : 1-8)

Here the festival of the first day of the seventh month
is associated with the ideas of renewal and firm resolve
to obey the Law of God which later became the domi-
nant themes of the festival. We read further that the
people, conscious as they were of their shortcomings,
were distressed to hear the words of the Law, but
Nehemiah, Ezra's companion, said to them:

*Go your way, eat the fat, and drink the sweet and send
portions unto him for whom nothing is prepared; for this
day is holy unto the Lord; neither be ye grieved; for the
joy of the Lord is your strength.* (*Neh.* viii : 10)

In the Rabbinic Literature

The *Mishnah*, the great code of Jewish Law compiled by
Rabbi Judah the Prince at the end of the second century,
speaks of four periods in the year, each of which is
known as *Rosh Ha-Shanah*. The first day of *Nisan*, for
instance, is the 'New Year for feasts' i.e. the festivals of
the Jewish year are counted from this day, as we have
seen. But the name *Rosh Ha-Shanah* is used mainly for
the festival which falls at the beginning of the seventh
month. R. Eliezer (second century) taught that the world

was created in *Tishri*. Although his contemporary, R. Joshua taught that the world was created in *Nisan*, the liturgy of *Rosh Ha-Shanah* follows R. Eliezer in speaking of the festival as the birthday of the world.

In addition to the Creation itself, various significant events in Jewish and world history are said to have occurred in this month. Abraham and Jacob were born in *Tishri* and they died in that month. It was in *Tishri* that Joseph was released from prison, and the bondage of our ancestors in Egypt came to an end, though they had to wait another six months before the actual deliverance. Sarah, Rachael and Hannah were remembered by God, that is, they were promised a child, in the month of *Tishri*.

For the Rabbis *Rosh Ha-Shanah* was the great day of judgment, ushering in the penitential season which culminates in the Day of Atonement. On *Rosh Ha-Shanah* all creatures pass before God 'like children of *Maron*'. The precise meaning of this expression, used in the *Mishnah*, is discussed by the later Rabbis. Some Rabbis connect the word *Maron* with the Aramaic word for 'sheep', yielding the idea, voiced in the well-known *Rosh Ha-Shanah* and *Yom Kippur* hymn, that God is the shepherd before whom all His flock pass on this day. Others remark that the reference is to a narrow ascent of a certain mountain where travellers were obliged to pass in single file. Others, again, connect the word *Maron* with a word meaning 'lordship' and interpret the phrase as referring to a legion of soldiers who pass in review before their commanding officer. All interpretations convey the same idea, of God surveying, as it were, the lives of all His creatures with an individual scrutiny. This theme, that *Rosh Ha-Shanah* demands honest self-searching by the *individual*, is found in many of the prayers of the day. It is true that Judaism holds the concept of the community as of the greatest importance— Judaism is the religion of the Jewish people—but *Rosh Ha-Shanah* reminds us that a community is composed of individuals, each with his own needs, desires, fears and hopes, and his own path in life which no one but he can tread. No two people are exactly alike in bodily form or features, say the Rabbis, and no two are alike in their thoughts and character. If the individual fails in self-realisation the community is deprived of that fraction of God's truth and God's light it was given only him or her to reveal.

The Name

There are four names of the festival found in the classical Jewish sources:

(1) *Rosh Ha-Shanah* (*Rosh*='the head of' or 'the beginning of', *Ha-Shanah*='the year'), the most popular of the four names.

(2) *Yom Teruah* ('The Day of Sounding the Horn'), the Biblical name for the festival.

(3) *Yom Ha-Din* ('Day of Judgment').

(4) *Yom Ha-Zikaron* ('Day of Remembrance'). On this day God 'remembers' His creatures. As of everything we say about God, when we use this expression we are resorting to symbolic language. God does not forget that He should require a period in which to remember.

7

Its meaning for us is that no deed or thought of man fails to bear fruit, for good or for ill, and that the life a man leads possesses permanent significance for him and for others. A famous *Hasidic* teacher said that in the *Rosh Ha-Shanah* prayers we speak of God as 'He who remembers the forgotten things', meaning that God remembers that which humans forget. The proud man, conscious only of the little good he has done, is forgetful of the wrongs he has committed, but God remembers the forgotten wrongs and forgets, as it were, the good so zealously recalled. But of the humble man, whose failings are ever before him, and who belittles his good deeds God says, 'He has forgotten but I will not forget!'

CHAPTER 2

THE LAWS AND CUSTOMS OF ROSH HA-SHANAH

Elul

ELUL, the last month of the old year, is hallowed by tradition as a period of preparation for the new. Rabbinic legend has it that Moses went up on to the mount to receive the second tablets of stone on the first day of this month and stayed there for forty days and forty nights until *Yom Kippur* when he brought down the Torah to his people. During these forty days Jewish tradition enjoins a special watchfulness and a special attention to the ideals of penitence, prayer and charity; albeit that the pursuit of these ideals is not to be limited to one period of the year.

As a reminder of the solemnity of these days the *Shophar* is sounded in the Synagogue at the end of the morning service (in some congregations at the evening service, too), with the exception of the day before *Rosh Ha-Shanah* when the *Shophar* is not sounded in order to make a clear distinction between the optional and the obligatory sounding.

Psalm Twenty-Seven

Psalm twenty-seven is recited morning and evening from the beginning of the month of *Elul* to the seventh day of the festival of *Sukkoth*. The usual reason given for this

9

choice is the Midrashic comment on the Psalm: ' "The Lord is my light" (verse i) on *Rosh Ha-Shanah*, "and my salvation" (verse i) on *Yom Kippur*, "For He concealeth me in His pavilion" (verse v) on *Sukkoth*.' But apart from this, the ideas of the Psalm make it most appropriate reading for the penitential season. Faith and trust in God, the desire 'to dwell in God's house', the plea to God to hear the prayer of the suppliant, the appeal to Him not to hide His face and to teach man His ways, all these are sentiments evoked by the introspective mood. The final verse, in particular, with its reminder of 'waiting for the Lord' is a powerful call to persistence in prayer. The Rabbis teach that if a man prays and his prayer is unanswered let him pray again, for the Psalmist says: 'Wait for the Lord; Be strong, and let thy heart take courage; Yea, wait thou for the Lord.'

Selichoth

As the days of *Elul* go by and *Rosh Ha-Shanah* draws near the mood of supplication becomes intensified. From the Sunday before *Rosh Ha-Shanah*, or the Sunday before that if *Rosh Ha-Shanah* falls on a Monday or Tuesday, special penitential prayers known as *Selichoth* (from a root meaning 'to pardon') are recited early in the morning before the statutory services. In addition to the days before *Rosh Ha-Shanah*, *Selichoth* are recited on the days between *Rosh Ha-Shanah* and *Yom Kippur*. During the bloodstained days of religious persecution in the Middle Ages the liturgical poets of Israel offered their laments to God, pleading for His mercies. The compositions of these men were collected and now form the major portion of the *Selichoth* prayers. Some of the *Selichoth* are earlier than the seventh century. The famous Prayer Book of Amram Gaon (*d.* 874) contains a number of *Selichoth*. *Selichoth* were composed in Italy, the Rhineland and France, in particular, and examples of the work of the liturgical poets residing in these lands are to be found in the present-day collection. The day before *Rosh Ha-Shanah* is known as *Zechor Brith* ('Remember the Covenant') after a prayer beginning with these words recalling the sacrifice of Isaac and the promise made to Abraham.

Visiting the Graves

It is a custom to visit the graves of parents during the month of *Elul*. This originated in the belief that the righteous dead intercede for the living before the throne of God. There are, however, obvious dangers to true religion in the notion of speaking to the dead while offering prayers. Consequently, many great Jewish teachers warn against any kind of direct prayer to the departed; the custom being observed rather as an act of filial piety in the remembrance of lives worthily lived.

Greetings

It is customary to greet one's friends on the first night of *Rosh Ha-Shanah* with the greeting: 'May you be inscribed (in the Book of Life) for a good year.' The Hebrew forms of the greeting according to the number and sex of the persons addressed are given in the Festival

Prayer Book. (R. 24). Tradition has it that after the first night of *Rosh Ha-Shanah* the greeting should be changed to '*gemar hatimah tobhah*': 'May you be *sealed* (in the Book of Life) for good.' This is based on the Rabbinic teaching that the names of the perfectly righteous are immediately recorded in the Book of Life. Consequently, to express the wish, after the first night of *Rosh Ha-Shanah* that a friend be *inscribed* in the Book of Life is to suggest that he is not perfectly righteous! Consideration for the feelings of others prompts a change in phraseology. The current English translation of *shanah tobhah* as 'happy year' is incorrect; the phrase means 'good year'. This is no mere pedantic insistence on the correct use of words, for the 'happy' year is the 'good' year. The citadel of happiness cannot be taken by storm. There is something pathetic in the assiduous search for happiness. All the great teachers are unanimous in suggesting that happiness and satisfaction in one's existence come of the life dedicated to self-transcending ideals. The happiest of men are those who allow themselves to be used for ideals greater than themselves. Judaism certainly does not teach that the road to Heaven is thorny and the road to Hell a primrose path. The desire for a good year is not only a worthier aim than the desire for a happy year but it embraces the latter in its comprehensiveness.

The Festive Meal

At the festive meal on the night of *Rosh Ha-Shanah* it is customary to dip a piece of bread, over which grace has been recited, in honey as a token of the sweet year to come. For the same reason a piece of apple is dipped in honey and eaten by all the participants, after which the prayer is recited: 'May it be Thy will, O Lord our God and God of our fathers, to renew unto us a good and pleasant year.' ('Good' and 'pleasant' are not always synonymous. At times the path of duty is hard and the way of ease delusory. We pray that in the year ahead we may find joy in leading the good life.) Apart from its sweetness the apple is a potent symbol in Jewish mysticism. The mystics interpret the red and white which are combined in the apple as symbols of the divine power and love uniting in harmony. Tradition has it that as many sweet things as possible should be eaten at this meal.

In some places a special point is made of eating fish, symbolising that our good deeds in the year ahead be as prolific as the numberless fish which swarm in the sea. Nuts should not be eaten on *Rosh Ha-Shanah* because, it is said, the Hebrew word for 'nut' has the same numerical value as the Hebrew word for 'sin'. The Talmudic Rabbis debate whether this kind of symbolism ought to be encouraged or whether it borders on the superstitious. The conclusion they come to is that these acts are good providing that they are looked upon as a reminder to man rather than as an attempt to influence by sympathetic magic. That is to say, the sweet things are not to be eaten in the belief that by doing so we automatically assure for ourselves a sweet year but as forceful reminders of the psychological benefits of beginning the year in an atmosphere of sweetness. The *Besht* (the founder of the *Hasidic* movement) was fond of quoting the verse: 'And when they came to Marah, they could not drink of the waters of Marah, for they were bitter.' (*Ex.* xv : 23) 'They were bitter,' said the *Besht*, refers not to the waters but to the people themselves! The bitter in soul will find bitterness everywhere; but all things contain sparks of holiness for the sweet of soul.

In some communities the loaves of bread for the festive meal on *Rosh Ha-Shanah* are baked in the form of ladders to symbolise the fortunes of men in the coming year, some descending the ladder of life, others ascending to the highest rungs of success and prosperity. The ladder recalls, too, the dream of Jacob, in which the patriarch saw the angels ascending and descending. The task of the descendants of Jacob is to create ladders linking earth to heaven.

Tashlich

The prophet Micah speaks of God casting the sins of Israel into the depths of the sea: 'He will again have compassion upon us; He will subdue our iniquities; and Thou wilt cast (*Ve-Tashlich*) all their sins into the depths of the sea.' (*Micah* vii : 19) On the basis of this verse the custom arose for Jews to go to a river on the first afternoon of *Rosh Ha-Shanah* (on the second afternoon if the first day falls on the Sabbath) there to recite this and other verses and various penitential hymns and prayers.

The Talmud contains no mention of *Tashlich*. The

first direct reference to the custom is in the writings of Jacob Mölln (d. 1425), the author of *Sepher Maharil*. Even if those scholars who detect a pagan origin for the custom are correct it is certain that Jewish teachers over the centuries have purged it of any offensive associations it may once have possessed. Various interpretations in the true spirit of Judaism have assimilated it to the best Jewish thought and idealism. Thus some see in the river a symbol of the primordial waters over which the spirit of God hovered, a reminder of the Creation. Others point to the *Midrash* which says that when Abraham went to offer up his son Isaac in obedience to God's command Satan assumed the guise of a river to bar his path. Abraham, undaunted, plunged into the river and went on his way, for no obstacles can deter the man of faith. Others again write that the fish in the river, whose eyes never close, symbolise the ever-watchful eye of God, open always to look down in mercy on His creatures. But when all has been said it remains true that many prominent teachers, like the Gaon of Vilna, preferred to ignore the *Tashlich* ceremony and spend the afternoon in Torah study or the recitation of Psalms.

The Ten Days of Penitence

'Seek ye the Lord while He may be found, Call ye upon Him while he is near.' (*Is.* lv : 6) This verse, implying that there is a time when the quest for God is particularly blessed with success, is applied by the Rabbis to the ten days from *Rosh Ha-Shanah* to *Yom Kippur*. That God is near to us at all times and that we can approach Him without having to wait for a special period of the year is basic to Jewish teaching. But there is much point in setting aside a portion of the year in which life is lived at a spiritual tempo well-nigh impossible for most people during the rest of the year. These days are known as the ten days of penitence, during which the good Jew and Jewess are expected to submit themselves to severe self-scrutiny in the effort to improve the quality of their lives. During this period special care should be taken in prayer and the other religious observances and, of course, special attention should be paid to consideration for the needs of others. The mystics note that apart from the two days of *Rosh Ha-Shanah* and the day of *Yom Kippur* there are seven days in this period, corresponding to the days of the week. By living at this time at the highest spiritual level of which one is capable the standard is set for all the other weeks of the year.

CHAPTER 3

THE ROSH HA-SHANAH PRAYERS

The Prayer Book

THE EARLIEST prayers in the Jewish Prayer Book go back to Temple times. The three features of the ancient service were the reading of the Law, the recitation of the *Shema*, and the silent prayer, recited while standing, the *Amidah* (from the root *amad*, 'to stand'). These have remained the central features of the Jewish service but hymns and prayers were added from time to time until the prayer book emerged in its present form. Each *Amidah* consists of three introductory and three concluding benedictions. These have the same form in every *Amidah* but the middle portion varies according to the occasion. Thus the middle portion for week-days consists mainly of a series of supplications while this portion on the Sabbaths and Festivals is devoted to the special nature of the day. The scope of this work does not allow for detailed commentary on those features which the *Rosh Ha-Shanah* liturgy shares with that of other days. The comments are limited to the specific *Rosh Ha-Shanah* prayers.

(*Note: To avoid duplication those hymns and prayers which are commented upon in the* Guide to Yom Kippur *are here marked with a cross reference. Page references in the following notes are to the Routledge and to the Shapiro, Vallentine editions of the Festival Prayer Book.*)

מַעֲרִיב

The Evening Service (R. 10-24, S. 12-28)

The evening service for *Rosh Ha-Shanah* is the statutory evening service consisting of the *Shema*, its benedictions, and the special *Rosh Ha-Shanah Amidah*, concluding with the *Alenu* prayer and the *Yigdal* hymn. On *Rosh Ha-Shanah* and *Yom Kippur* and the days between these festivals the words 'the holy *King*' are substituted in the *Amidah* for 'the holy *God*'. (R. 16, S. 21 and freq.) During this period the worshipper's mind is directed to the concept of God as King whose loyal subjects renew their allegiance. As the Talmud puts it: 'Throughout the year one says "The holy God", and "King who lovest righteousness and judgment", except during the ten days between New Year and the Day of Atonement, when he says, "The holy King" and "The King of judgment".' During this period, too, four short prayers for life are added to the *Amidah* at appropriate pauses. These additions were introduced in the period of the *Geonim*, who flourished from the end of the sixth century. The first of these is: 'Remember us unto life, O King, who delightest in life, and inscribe us in the book of life, for thine own sake, O living God.' (R. 15, S. 19 and freq.) This prayer is inserted in the first benediction of the *Amidah* because in that benediction, too, God is entreated to help man for 'the sake of His name'. The Jew loves life but he prays that life be given him in order that he may serve his Maker. The second addition is: 'Who is like unto Thee, Father of mercy, Who in mercy rememberest Thy creatures unto life.' (R. 15, S. 19 and freq.) This is inserted in the second benediction of the *Amidah* because of the association of the word 'mercy' which occurs in both the benediction and the additional prayer. The third addition: 'And inscribe all the children of Thy covenant for a good life' (R. 18, S. 24 and freq.), is inserted in the penultimate benediction of the *Amidah* because of the association of the word 'good' which occurs in both the benediction and the additional prayer. Finally the addition: 'In the book of life, blessing, peace and good sustenance may we be remembered and inscribed before Thee, we and all Thy people the house of Israel, for a happy life and peace' (R. 18, S. 24 and freq.), is inserted in the last benediction of the *Amidah* because of the association of the word 'peace' which occurs in both the benediction and the additional prayer.

וּבְכֵן תֵּן פַּחְדְּךָ

Now Therefore, O Lord our God, Impose Thine Awe (R. 15-16, S. 20 and freq.)

This long prayer for the establishment of the Kingdom of Heaven on earth is recited as part of every *Amidah* on *Rosh Ha-Shanah* and *Yom Kippur*. The prayer is very old, its exact origin is unknown, but it is generally associated with the famous Babylonian teacher, *Rab* (on whom see the further note to *Malkhuyoth, Zikhronoth* and *Sho-pharoth* p. 28). In magnificent Hebrew, reminiscent of the language power of the prophets, the prayer looks forward to the day when evil will be banished from the earth and all men will unite to do God's will. The accusation that Judaism is narrow and particularistic is nowhere more effectively challenged. At the beginning of the year when the Jew comes before his God his thoughts are not for himself alone, nor for his people alone, but that the blessing of peace be granted to all mankind and that God reign supreme. The phrase: 'and all wickedness shall be wholly consumed like smoke,' follows in the tradition of the wise Jewish woman, the wife of Rabbi Meir (second century), who taught that one should never pray for the downfall of the wicked but for the destruction of wickedness.

מְלוֹךְ עַל כָּל הָעוֹלָם כֻּלוֹ

Reign Over the Whole Universe (R. 17, S. 22 and freq.)

This ancient benediction is part of each *Amidah* on *Rosh Ha-Shanah*. Its theme, like that of so many other prayers of the day, is God as King. There is a nice comment on the Hebrew opening of this prayer which really means: 'Reign over the whole of all the Universe'. Because, it is said, in Jewish teaching a majority is treated as the whole; if, for instance, a majority of scholars favour a certain ruling the decision is given in their favour as if all the scholars were agreed. But the Jew is not content that the majority of men recognise God. He prays that God may reign over *the whole of all* the Universe, he cannot rest until the idols are shattered and God alone is King. But, Jewish teachers remind us, world betterment must start with self betterment. Sublime though the idea of God's universal reign is, Jewish teaching is insistent that we start with ourselves.

תִּקְעוּ בַחֹדֶשׁ שׁוֹפָר

Blow Ye the Trumpet (R. 14, S. 19)

Before the evening *Amidah* verses four and five of Psalm *eighty-one* are recited. The word translated as 'in the time appointed'—Hebrew, *bakkeseh*—is connected by the Rabbis with a root meaning 'to cover'. Every other festival of the Jewish year occurs at a time when the moon can be seen but *Rosh Ha-Shanah*, which falls at the beginning of the month, is the festival 'when the moon is covered'.

שַׁחֲרִית

The Morning Service

The morning service for *Rosh Ha-Shanah* is composed of the usual Sabbath and Festival prayers, hymns and benedictions with the appropriate Torah readings. After the reading of the *Haphtorah*, the *Shophar* is sounded. The *Musaph Amidah* is the longest *Amidah* of the year. Special *Rosh Ha-Shanah* hymns and prayers have been added through the ages and now form part of the liturgy of the day. The more important of these will here be considered.

מֶלֶךְ אָזוּר גְּבוּרָה

King with Might Begirded (R. 81, S. 100)

Eleazar Kalir, the author of this hymn, was one of the

greatest of the Hebrew liturgical poets but so little is known of his background that scholars have been unable to discover with any degree of certainty the period in which he flourished or the place where he lived. Most authorities think that he lived some time between 700 and 900 C.E. The stanza: 'King in tenfold garments' is based on the Midrashic teaching that Scripture, in ten places, speaks of God calling Israel His bride and in ten places speaks of Israel praising God as clothed in the garments of strength, majesty and righteousness. The Kabbalists, in particular, dwell on the Ten *Sephiroth*, the ten divine attributes of love and power, which are as garments to the *En Soph*, the Infinite, the hidden, unknown essence of the Deity. The idea behind all such descriptions is that though God's essence can never be comprehended by man He can nonetheless be known by man through the manifestations of His presence in human life and history and in the beauty and majesty of the external world. Each verse of the hymn, after the word *melekh*, begins with a letter of the Hebrew alphabet, from *'Aleph*, the first letter, to *Tav*, the last.

כְּבוֹדוֹ אֹהֶל כְּהַיּוֹם

Tent-like This Day (R. 86, S. 105)

Another alphabetic acrostic by Eleazar Kalir praising God as King. The stanza: 'Ah, pity us, by grace of our descent' speaks of the merits of the patriarchs. 'Him to whom three messengers were sent' is Abraham who was visited by the three angels. 'Him for whom the angel's tears were spent' is Isaac for whom, says the *Midrash*, the angels shed tears as he was bound on the altar. 'Him who down in sleep his body cast, Where up and down the angels passed' is Jacob who saw in his dream the ladder linking heaven and earth. The references to the angels are particularly apt at this stage of the morning service which dwells poetically on the song of the Heavenly hosts.

יֵרֵאתִי בִּפְצוֹתִי

Trembling I Now Pour Forth (R. 95, S. 118)
The Reader's prayer of supplication before he repeats the *Amidah* in which he prays that God give him strength to offer supplication on behalf of the congregation whose deputy he is. The author has signed his name, Yekuthiel b. Moses (of Speyer, eleventh century), in an acrostic. The first letters of each half-sentence combine to form the words: 'May Yekuthiel ben Moses be strong and of good courage. Let him live'.

Thou art our God (R. 98, S. 122)
See *Guide to Yom Kippur* p. 39.

שְׁמוֹ מְפָאֲרִים עֲדַת חֲבָלוֹ

His Chosen People Glorify His Name (R.99, S. 123)

The first verses of this hymn, ending with the word *kadosh*, 'most holy', all contain the author's name—Simeon ben Isaac ben Abun of Mayence (eleventh century). The other verses are in the form of an alphabetical acrostic. Simeon b. Isaac, also known as Simeon the

23

Great, was renowned in the Middle Ages as a Talmudist, liturgical poet and miracle worker. Legend tells of three marvellous mirrors he possessed through which he could see the past and the future. Simeon lived in a period of fierce religious persecutions and such was the fury of the oppressor that for a time Jews were expelled from Mayence for their refusal to be baptised. Largely as a result of Simeon's intervention the persecution was halted and Jews were permitted to return to Mayence which became a great centre of Jewish learning. (Simeon's famous contemporary at Mayence, Gershom, the 'Light of the Exile', convened a Synod at which polygamy was officially banned.) The grateful community perpetuated Simeon's memory by mentioning his name every Sabbath in the Synagogue in a prayer for the repose of his soul. Despite the sufferings of his people, Simeon's hymn breathes love for all men and expresses the author's yearning that 'all creatures of the Universe, all denizens of earth' will proclaim that God reigns.

אַדִּירֵי אֲיָמָה

The Terrible Sons (R. 105-6, S. 128)

An alphabetic acrostic on the song of the angels by Kalir. The first two words of each verse begin with the letters of the alphabet from 'Aleph to Tav and the letter is repeated in the third word of the verse. Scripture speaks of God as He who was King, He who is King and He who shall be King, hence the threefold refrain.

Unto God Who Ordereth Judgment (R. 106, S. 130)

See *Guide to Yom Kippur* p. 41.

(*Note: before the comments on the second half of the Rosh Ha-Shanah morning service a few comments are here made on the early morning service for the second day.*)

מֶלֶךְ אָמוֹן

O King, Thy Word (R. 177-179, S. 237-240)

An alphabetic acrostic by Simeon ben Isaac ben Abun based on the three great themes of *Rosh Ha-Shanah*—God as King, God as He who remembers, and the sounding of the Shophar. In this and other hymns of Simeon there are references to his name by means of ingenious acrostics, also to the name of his son, Elhanan (see particularly the verse on p. 178 R., S. 238, beginning *El Hanan*), of whom a curious medieval legend is told. Simeon's son, Elhanan, being taken away from his father in his infancy and educated as a Christian, made rapid strides in the knowledge of his new faith and eventually became Pope! After a visit by his father, who convinced him of the truth of the Jewish faith, the Pope openly abjured Christianity and returned to the faith of his fathers for which he suffered a martyr's death. His father immortalised his son's memory by recording his name in liturgical compositions.

אָתִיתִי לְחַנְנֶךְ

I Come to Supplicate (R. 190-191, S. 254-255)

The Reader's supplication for the second day is in the

form of an alphabetic acrostic by Simeon ben Isaac ben Abun, with the name Simeon in acrostic at the end of the prayer. The suppliant protests that he is utterly unworthy of mouthing the praises of God on behalf of his people. He comes before the awful majesty of God's Throne like a beggar at the gates. The *Zohar* remarks that Scripture speaks of 'the prayer of Moses', 'the prayer of David' and 'the prayer of the poor', but the greatest of these is the prayer of the poor who comes before God without any claim to merit and throws himself on the divine mercy.

שְׁלַחְתִּי בְּמַלְאֲכוּת

I Am Sent (R. 193-194, S. 258-260)

An ingenious acrostic by Simeon ben Isaac ben Abun. Each verse of the hymn has four parts each beginning with the same letter. These letters spell out four times— *Simeon bar* (= 'son of' in Aramaic) *Yitzhak*.

מֶלֶךְ עֶלְיוֹן

King, Most High (R. 201-202, S. 269-271)

Another hymn in acrostic form by Simeon ben Isaac ben Abun. Each verse begins with an alternate letter of the alphabet and the author's name is contained in the last stanza. The hymn contrasts the splendour and majesty of the 'King, Most High' with the lowliness of man 'King on earth'. This hymn has been criticised for its poor opinion of man, robbing him of his dignity. This is to misunderstand the author's purpose: it is puny, insignificant man who recognises the majesty of God.

The mood is not one of lament nor melancholic **abase-**ment but of exhilaration in the presence of the Source of all being. Man is taken beyond himself and as a result is elevated into a realm where he ceases to be insignificant. The hymn can, without distortion of its meaning, be read as an ecstatic commentary to the Rabbinic teaching that wherever the greatness of God is found there, too, is found His humility.

כָּל שִׂנְאֲנֵי שַׁחַק

All the Hosts of Heaven (R. 203-204, S. 271-274) The theme of this hymn by Simeon ben Isaac ben Abun is that the heavenly hosts unite with man in singing God's praises. That man is greater than the angels because he lives in an imperfect world and can yet rise to the heights is a constant theme in the Rabbinic tradition. The angels, say the Rabbis, cannot sing their song above until Israel sings its song down below. Simeon's pattern is obviously the hymn of Kalir for the first day, 'The terrible sons'. (R. 105-106, S. 128-130) The second half of each verse begins with a letter of the alphabet.

Our Father, Our King (R. 111-113, 210-212, S. 143-146, 281-284)
See *Guide to Yom Kippur* p. 36.

The Additional Prayer (R. 131-142, S. 169-184) The Additional *Amidah* for *Rosh Ha-Shanah* is more than a prayer, it contains the most sublime thoughts on God and His relationship to man; it is a summary of the Jewish faith and its cosmic significance in which are heard the accents of law-giver, prophet and saint. The central feature of this *Amidah* is the recitation of Scriptural verses on the themes of divine Kingship, Remembrance and the sounding of the *Shophar*, each set of verses followed by an appropriate benediction. The three sets are known as *Malkhuyoth* (verses of Sovereignty), *Zikhronoth* (verses of Remembrance) and *Shopharoth* (verses dealing with the *Shophar*).

The arrangements of verses and benedictions in this form is very old but the order as we have it today (probably with some later additions) was composed by the famed Babylonian teacher, Rab (d. C.E. 247). Rab was born in Babylon, where Jews had lived for centuries and where they had risen to positions of power and affluence in the Persian Empire. Though mainly wealthy, and while playing its full share in maintaining Palestinian institutions and intensely loyal to Judaism, the Jewish Community in Babylon was not noted for its scholarship. Rab, like so many other keen students, left his home to sit at the feet of the renowned Palestinian teachers, particularly Rabbi Judah the Prince, the editor of the *Mishnah*, whose favourite pupil he became. Returning to Babylon, Rab stirred the intellectual sloth of his people. For more than eight hundred years Babylon became the foremost centre of Jewish learning in the world and this was attributed by later generations to the initial efforts of Rab. It was said that he found an open field and fenced it around. A giant of a man, physically as well as mentally so that he was given the nickname 'The Tall', he compelled the respect and reverence of his contemporaries and of subsequent generations. Among his sayings is that in the life to come there will be no eating or drinking, no procreation, no enmity or hatred, no competition, but the righteous will sit with their crowns on their heads basking in the radiance of the Divine Presence. Rab's family claimed descent from Shimei, the brother of King David. From the prayers he composed it can be seen that, in some measure, the mantle of the 'sweet singer in Israel' had, indeed, fallen upon him.

The Hebrew Bible is divided into three parts, *Torah*, the five books of Moses, *Nebhiim*, 'The Prophets', the prophetical and historical books, and *Kethubhim*, 'The Sacred Writings', Psalms, Proverbs, Job and so forth. This division is followed in the *Malkhuyoth*, *Zikhronoth* and *Shopharoth* arrangement. The structure of each of these is first a hymn of adoration, expressing the idea of Sovereignty, Remembrance or the *Shophar*, followed by Biblical texts on the same theme. These texts are ten in number, the first three from the *Torah*, the second three from the *Kethubhim* (actually from the Psalms), and the third set of three from the *Nebhiim*, followed by a final *Torah* text. Each set of ten concludes with an appropriate benediction. The whole structure of the Additional *Amidah* is as follows:

(1) The first three benedictions (with which every *Amidah* begins). (R. 131-133, S. 169-171)

(2) The prayers for the restoration of the Temple Service. (R. 133-134, S. 172-173)

(3) The introductory hymn for *Malkhuyoth*. (R. 135-136, S. 174-175)

(4) The ten 'proof-texts' for *Malkhuyoth*. (R. 135-136, S. 175)

(5) The concluding *Malkhuyoth* benediction. (R. 136, S. 176)

(6) The introductory *Zikhronoth* hymn. (R. 136-138, S. 176-179)

(7) The *Zikhronoth* 'proof-texts'. (R. 137-138, S. 177-179)

(8) The concluding *Zikhronoth* benediction. (R. 138-139, S. 178-179)

(9) The introductory *Shopharoth* hymn. (R. 139, S. 179)

(10) The *Shopharoth* 'proof-texts'. (R. 139-140, S. 179-181)

(11) The concluding *Shopharoth* benediction. (R. 140, S. 181)

(12) The final three benedictions (with which every *Amidah* concludes). (R. 140-141, S. 181-183)

Here is the place to examine each of the three main sections in greater detail.

(a) Malkhuyoth

Malkhuyoth begins with the *Alenu* hymn which became so popular that it was used as the concluding hymn of every service. Here the balance between Israel's particularism and its universalistic hope is given classical expression. Israel gives thanks that it is not a heathen people without knowledge of God's ways but, far from seeking the exclusive enjoyment of God's favour, waits for the day when the whole world is 'set under the kingdom of the Almighty' and when 'all the children of flesh will call upon Thy Name'.

The 'proof-texts' from the *Torah*, pointing to Israel's recognition of God as King, are *Ex.* xv : 18, *Num.* xxiii : 21 and *Deut.* xxxiii : 5. The three texts from Psalms are xxii : 29, xciii : 1 and xxiv : 7-10. The theme is repeated in the three texts from the Prophets, introduced by the words: 'And by the hands of thy servants, the prophets, it is written'. The texts are *Isaiah* xliv : 6, *Obadiah* i : 21 and *Zech.* xiv : 9. The final *Torah* text is the *Shema*, Israel's great declaration of faith, *Deut.* vi : 4. The concluding benediction is used for all the other *Amidahs* of *Rosh Ha-Shanah*.

(b) Zikhronoth

Zikhronoth begins with a hymn of praise to God who remembers all things. In this hymn, too, the universalistic note is predominant. Nations great and small, as well as the individual, pass before God. Reference is made to Noah who was saved from the waters of the flood and the prayer is offered that 'his seed (i.e. the whole human race) be increased as the dust of the earth and his offspring as the sand of the sea.' In Rabbinic thought non-Jews are called 'the sons of Noah'. The official view of the Synagogue has long been that the righteous of all nations have a share in the life to come. The degree of righteousness demanded is observance of the seven precepts given to the sons of Noah. There are various classifications of these basic rules of decent human

conduct but the following is the one generally accepted:
(1) The prohibition of idolatry; (2) The prohibition of
blasphemy; (3) The prohibition of murder; (4) The prohibition of adultery and incest; (5) The prohibition of
theft; (6) The prohibition of eating a limb torn from a
living animal; (7) The duty of providing an adequate
system of justice in the State.

The first *Torah* 'proof-text' is *Gen.* viii : 1, followed
by *Ex.* ii : 24 and *Lev.* xxvi : 42. The *Kethubhim* texts
are *Psalms* cxi : 4 and 5 and cvi : 45. The three prophetic
texts are *Jeremiah* ii : 2 in which God lovingly recalls
Israel's loyalty in its youth, *Ezekiel* xvi : 60, and the
exquisitely tender comparison of Ephraim to a precious
son whose father's heart is moved to compassion by the
mere mention of his name, *Jeremiah* xxxi : 20. Here the
final *Torch* text is quoted in the benediction in which
particular reference is made to the binding of Isaac and
the covenant made by God.

(c) Shopharoth

Shopharoth begins with a hymn in praise of the Revelation on Sinai when the sound of the *Shophar* was heard.
The three *Torah* texts are all taken from the account of
the Revelation in the book of *Exodus*. (xix : 16, xix : 19
and xx : 15) Four texts are quoted from *Psalms*, xlvii : 6,
xcviii : 6, lxxxi : 4 and the whole of *Psalm* cl. The
prophetic texts all have reference to the Messianic age
foretold by the prophets when the great *Shophar* will be
sounded to usher in a new world. The texts are *Isaiah*
xviii : 3, xxvii : 13 and *Zech.* ix : 14. Here, again, the

final *Torah* text is quoted in the final benediction. (It is probable that with regard to *Malkhuyoth* the final *Torah* text is quoted *before* the benediction because this benediction, as we have seen, (p. 20) is not confined to the Additional *Amidah*. Perhaps, it was felt to be more fitting to leave this benediction without any special reference to the Additional *Amidah* so that it could be used for the other *Amidahs* of the day.) The final *Torah* text is *Numbers* x : 10 and the benediction looks forward to its fulfilment in the days of the Messiah.

וּנְתַנֶּה תֹּקֶף

We Will Celebrate (R. 146-147, S. 191-192).

וְכֹל מַאֲמִינִים

And All Believe (R. 149-151, S. 197-200)

וְיֶאֱתָיוּ כֹל לְעָבְדֶּךָ

And All the World Shall Come (R. 151-152, S. 201-202)

עָלֵינוּ

Alenu (R. 154, S. 205)

See *Guide to Yom Kippur* pp. 46-49.

CHAPTER 4

THE TORAH AND HAPHTORAH
READINGS

The Torah Reading for the First Day (R. 117-119, S. 151-155)

THE *Torah* reading for the first day of *Rosh Ha-Shanah* is the twenty-first chapter of the book of Genesis, dealing with Isaac's birth, his growth to manhood, Abraham's banishment of his son Ishmael, and Abraham's peace treaty with Abimelech. The reason generally given for this choice is the tradition that Isaac was born on *Rosh Ha-Shanah*. Professor Büchler has, however, advanced an ingenious theory to account for the choice. In ancient Palestine it was the custom to read in the Synagogue each week smaller portions of the *Torah* than we do now so that three, instead of one, years elapsed from the beginning of the *Torah* reading to its completion. Our present practice follows the ancient Babylonian practice of completing the *Torah* in one year. Now Büchler has shown that in the earlier triennial cycle the portion for *Rosh Ha-Shanah* was, once every three years, this twenty-first chapter of Genesis. In later ages, though the Babylonian custom was well-nigh universally adopted, the original reading was retained for *Rosh Ha-Shanah*.

There is the further consideration that this chapter comes immediately before the account of the binding of Isaac, read on the second day of *Rosh Ha-Shanah*. As we

34

have seen, this is one of the great themes of the festival. As the story of the binding of Isaac was obviously appropriate reading for the day what could be more natural than to choose as supplementary reading the account of Isaac's birth in the previous chapter? (Büchler, on the other hand, suggests that the account of Isaac's binding was read on the second day because it follows, in the Bible, the account of his birth read on the first day!)

The name *Isaac* is connected in this and in other Biblical passages with the Hebrew root *tzahak* meaning 'to laugh'. In the context this has the connotation of 'mocking laughter'. To their contemporaries, even to themselves, there was something absurd about the birth of a child to Abraham and Sarah, this man and woman of advanced years. Jewish teachers have read into the account an anticipation of the fate of Isaac's descendants, the people of Israel. The very birth of this people was a miracle, who but a Moses, under divine aid, could have succeeded in welding a rabble of slaves into a great nation? In subsequent Jewish history it seemed on more than one occasion that the Jews were doomed to extinction. The mocking laughter which attended the birth of Isaac re-echoed at the destruction of the first and second Temples, at the expulsion from Spain, and, in our own day, in Nazi-dominated Europe. But always the laughter was silenced to wonder as bruised Israel survived to rebuild its life in new surroundings.

The Hagar narrative has received a good deal of attention from Jewish commentators. The Rabbis say that Hagar was an Egyptian princess who, hearing the world-shattering truths taught of the God of justice, righteousness and holiness by Abraham, left the glories of her father's court to become a maid-servant in the home of the man she revered. Apart from their religious value, the stories of the Patriarchs in the book of Genesis belong to the highest examples of the literary art. Powerful ideas are conveyed with an astonishing economy of words. In the Hagar story, for instance, the Hebrew word for 'bow' occurs twice. When she thinks that her child will die Hagar casts him in despair under a shrub and sits apart 'at the distance of a bow-shot'. When the child is saved and grows to manhood he becomes an archer, 'a wielder of the *bow*'. It is as if the narrative seeks to remind us of the importance of the home background in the training of children. The mother for whom, at a terrible crisis in her life, the bow is the most potent symbol, will rear a child who wields the bow!

There is a significant *Midrashic* comment on the verse: 'God heard the voice of the lad where he is'. The *Midrash* imagines the angels protesting: 'How can Ishmael be spared in that his descendants will torment Israel?'; God replies: 'At this moment he is worthy to be saved'; God hears the voice of the lad *where he is*. Man is a creature of moods and cannot live ever on the heights. The firm resolves he makes on *Rosh Ha-Shanah* may weaken when the days of self-examination are gone. But at least, the Rabbis might have said, let man's purpose be strong on these days that God might hear his voice *where he is*.

Abraham, in the Jewish tradition, is the man of compassion, sitting at the door of his tent ready to welcome the hungry and needy. On the verse: 'Abraham planted a tamarisk tree (*'eshel*) in Beer-sheba and called there on the name of the Lord, the everlasting God', the Rabbis remark that the initial letters of the word *'eshel* represent the Hebrew words for 'eating', 'drinking' and 'accompanying on the way'. Abraham, say the Rabbis, loved to provide all men with their basic needs irrespective of their way of life. Those he benefited were generally so impressed that they cast aside their idols to become worshippers of the true God. Religion has all too often suffered severe set-backs because of the repellent quality of some of its representatives. The Abrahamic ideal is that of the religious man of goodwill who brings men to God by his simple goodness.

The Maphtir for the First and Second Days
(R. 120 and 219, S. 155 and 292)

On both the first and second days of *Rosh Ha-Shanah* the *Maphtir* is the portion of the book of Numbers (xxix : 1-6) describing the special offerings of the day. *Rosh Ha-Shanah*, falling as it does at the beginning of the seventh month, is always, in addition, the New Moon festival. Hence the references in this portion to the New Moon offerings.

The Haphtorah for the First Day (R. 121-123, S. 156-160)

The prophetic reading for the first day is the first part of the book of Samuel (*I Sam.* i : 1 to ii : 10) describing

Hannah's passionate plea for the gift of a son and her hymn of triumph and joy when the prayer was answered. Apart from the tradition that it was on *Rosh Ha-Shanah* that Hannah's prayer was heard, this portion was chosen because of its link with the *Torah* reading. Both Sarah and Hannah are blessed with a son when it had seemed that they were destined to be barren. It is a happy coincidence that the mother, who brings the child to birth, should be celebrated in the readings chosen for the festival of creation, the birthday of the world. The tender love of the Jewish mother for her child and her complete, self-sacrificing devotion has been the constant theme of our poets and singers. Even the love of God is, in a memorable passage, described in terms of a mother's love for her child: 'Like one whom his mother comforteth, so will I comfort you' (*Is.* lxvi : 13), refuting the allegation that Judaism is a masculine religion which speaks in but halting accents to women.

Hannah prays silently, she 'speaks in her heart', only her lips move and her voice is not heard. From which the Rabbis infer that true prayer is in the heart and that though the words of prayer should be clearly enunciated they should not be uttered so loudly as to be overheard by others.

The Torah reading for the Second Day (R. 216-218, S. 289-292)

On the second day the twenty-second chapter of Genesis (1-24) is read. This deals mainly with the binding of Isaac. Abraham is commanded by God to take his be-

loved son, Isaac, in whom are centred all his hopes for
the future, and to offer him up as a sacrifice on one of
the mountains. Abraham obeys the voice of God. He
rises early in the morning, taking the lad with him.
Gradually he reveals his dread purpose. Isaac accepts his
fate willingly and allows his father to bind him on the
altar. Abraham takes the knife in his hand to perform the
deed but an angel calls to him from heaven bidding him
to stay his hand. A ram is discovered in the thicket and
this is substituted for Isaac. God promises Abraham that
because he has done this thing his seed will be blessed
and be a blessing to mankind.

Such is the story and it has been given two kinds of
interpretation. Many have seen the chief value of the
story as a dramatic protest against the cruel heathen
notion that the wrath of the gods could be averted by
child sacrifice. According to this interpretation, the
really significant part of the narrative is the angel's call
to Abraham that he stay his hand. A new conception of
religious worship was given to Abraham, that the true
God does not require the death of his followers. It is
their lives he wants.

In modern times, chiefly under the influence of the
Danish thinker, Kierkegaard, whose doctrine of the need
for 'commitment' to religious truth has won many
adherents, another interpretation, found, too, in many
of the Jewish sources, has gained ground. In this view it
is not the 'happy ending' that is significant but the
willingness of Abraham to obey the voice of God even
when it appeared to command that which would have

the effect of setting at naught all that God's revelation had meant to Abraham. God had promised Abraham that a great nation would spring from Isaac, ready to spread among all men the truth Abraham had recognised. And now Abraham hears the voice of God demanding not alone the complete frustration of this hope but a foul immoral act from which Abraham's noble spirit recoils. Yet despite the anguish of his heart Abraham hastens to obey the call. The test of the strength of a man's religious convictions depends on his preparedness to act on them in offering up his most cherished values in their behalf. Religious faith is not with ease acquired: it is the profound sense of conviction born of the tensions, contradictions and the very despair of life.

This second interpretation is popular today because man's stresses during the past decades have had the result of making him dissatisfied with an easy-going faith. Many have felt that if the voice of God is to be heard at all today it must be through the bitter struggle of a painful tormented existence. The tendency has been to turn the famous Browning poem upside down, to declare that because all's wrong with the world God's in His Heaven. Only out of the depths can man call upon the Lord.

It would seem that in the best Jewish tradition both interpretations are combined. The anguish of Abraham is vividly depicted in the Rabbinic legend of Satan subtly whispering in his ear: 'Yesterday He said: "For in Isaac shall thy seed be called" and now He says: "Take now thy son and offer him for a burnt offering" '. The

Rabbis speak of the *Akedah* (from the root 'to bind') as the greatest 'test' to which Abraham was subjected. And the prayers of *Rosh Ha-Shanah* recall the merit of Abraham who 'suppressed his compassion in order to perform Thy will with a perfect heart'—the man renowned for his pity prepared to carry out a pitiless act. But, on the other hand, the 'happy ending' is no sentimental afterthought depriving the whole episode of its grandeur. For the God of Israel is the God of life and the whole point of the ending is that He did not, in fact, require the death of Isaac. To emphasise the ending to the exclusion of Abraham's willingness to follow the voice of God wherever it led is to reduce the whole narrative to a rather superficial homily on the sacredness of human life. But to ignore the ending is to invite a jaundiced view of religion which exalts the anti-rational in man's soul and acquires depth at the expense of a healthy, normal outlook on life.

Tradition has it that the mount on which Isaac was bound became in later years the site of the temple. The *Hasidim* tell of one of their masters who once paid greater honour to a young man of deep, sincere piety and goodness than to a famous scholar. Explaining his conduct, the master pointed out that the Temple was not built on Sinai, the mount on which the *Torah* was revealed, but on Moriah where a man, Abraham, once showed the extent to which self-abnegation can go.

The chapter concludes with the prosaic list of the children born to Abraham's brother. This comes as an anti-climax after the story of the *Akedah*. The Rabbis explain the connection by noting that the list of names contains that of Rebekah who became Isaac's wife. She was a suitable partner in life for the man who had been prepared to lay down his life for his God. Later homiletic fancy suggested that this passage is appropriate reading for *Rosh Ha-Shanah* because the initial letters of the last name in the list, *Maakhah*, form the words *melekh'al kol ha-olam*, 'King of the whole universe'.

The Haphtorah for the Second Day (R. 219-220, S. 293-295)

The *Haphtorah* for the second day is taken from the book of Jeremiah (xxxi : 2-20). This portion concludes with the verses: 'Is Ephraim my dear son? is he a pleasant child? For as often as I speak against him, I do earnestly remember him still. . . ', a fitting choice of reading for the festival of remembrance. (As we have seen, these verses are quoted among the 'proof texts' in the *Zikhronoth* portion of the *Amidah*.)

In this portion, too, the *motif* of motherly love is found. The matriarch, Rachael, is described as weeping for her exiled children, to be assured by God that they will be restored to the land of their fathers.

CHAPTER 5

THE SHOPHAR

The Shophar

THE *Shophar* is one of the earliest musical instruments known to man. Fashioned from the horn of an animal it could easily be manufactured and was extensively used in ancient times. In the Bible there are frequent references to the use of the *Shophar*. The actual meaning of the word is not certain. Some have understood the root *Shophar* as meaning 'to be bright', a reference to the sharp, piercing notes of the instrument. Others again have connected the root with the idea of hollowing out. From the earliest times the *Shophar* was fashioned from an animal's horn. In the story of the priests marching round Jericho until its walls collapsed to the sound of the *Shophar*, Scripture records: 'And it shall be, that when they make a long blast *with the ram's horn*, and when ye hear the sound of the *Shophar*. . .', clear evidence that the two are synonymous.

According to the Rabbis the horn of any clean animal (i.e. an animal Jews may eat), sheep, goat or antelope, is fit to be used as a *Shophar* on *Rosh Ha-Shanah* but preference is given to the ram's horn because of the substitution of a ram for the lad in the story of the binding of Isaac. The only exception made by the Rabbis was the horn of the cow because Israel had once worshipped the golden calf and it was considered unfitting that Israel appear before God on the great day of judgment with an instrument which would recall that severe lapse from loyalty. In the words of the Rabbis: 'A prosecutor cannot act as a defender'. For the same reason, say the Rabbis, the High Priest doffed his golden garments and entered the Holy of Holies on *Yom Kippur* clad only in white. (The medieval moralistic work, *Sepher Hasidim*, applies the principle that a prosecutor cannot act as defender to forbid the sounding of the *Shophar* by a quarrelsome man notorious for his fault-finding.)

Why We Blow the Shophar

Why are we commanded to blow the *Shophar* on *Rosh Ha-Shanah*? What do the *Shophar* notes represent? Are spiritual truths expressed in this ritual? Before dealing with these questions it is important to consider how Jewish tradition has discovered meaning in those Biblical precepts for which no reason is given in Scripture.

There is a wealth of teaching on this subject. Some Jewish authorities tended to discourage the search for reasons about matters on which the *Torah* is silent. In the opinion of these teachers such commands as the dietary laws were given as a test of man's obedience. Man with his finite, human mind cannot hope to penetrate the mystery of the divine will. The devout Jew will, therefore, submit to what appears to be an arbitrary rule in the spirit of love for God who ordained it and faith in His wisdom. Other teachers of note were not content with this approach. They believed that the precepts of the *Torah* are carried out with far greater warmth and enthusiasm when the reason for their observance is known. Furthermore, they felt obliged to demonstrate that the basic wisdom and humanity of the *Torah* is revealed in all its precepts, and they were convinced that if only man made the effort to understand he would grasp the inner meaning of the most obscure details. It is undoubtedly true that in some religious problems the voice of curiosity must be silenced because we are in the presence of the mysterious and unfathomable. But in our questing age only a tiny minority is likely to be impressed with this reply to all religious problems. It is right and proper, therefore, to examine here in detail the various reasons for the command to blow the *Shophar*. They are found in the Rabbinic literature and in the writings of the Jewish philosophers and mystics.

It is not necessary to assume that all the reasons given are historical. Some of them are quite obviously attempts at reading later ideas into the Biblical text. But the ideas behind the 'reasons' are all in accord with the spirit of Judaism.

David ben Joseph Abudraham quotes, in his work on the liturgy written in 1340, ten reasons for sounding the *Shophar* which he attributes to the famous Babylonian teacher, Saadia Gaon, who died at the age of fifty in 942. (Saadia was fond of classification by number and the number ten has featured prominently in Jewish symbolism from the earliest times.) The ten reasons of Saadia are:

(1) God is acclaimed as King on the New Year. It is customary to blow trumpets at the king's coronation

and by sounding the *Shophar* we express our desire to become loyal subjects of the divine King.

(2) *Rosh Ha-Shanah* is the beginning of the Ten Days of Penitence, when humans are obliged to search their hearts and return to God. The *Shophar* blasts herald the beginning of this period.

(3) The *Torah* was given on Sinai accompanied by the sound of the *Shophar*. On the new year festival we re-enact the greatest event in Jewish history and resolve to be faithful to the teachings of the *Torah*.

(4) The prophets compare their admonitions to the sound of the *Shophar*. On *Rosh Ha-Shanah* we remind ourselves of those ancient teachings by which the life of mankind was ennobled and which are still of the utmost relevance to man's predicament.

(5) The Temple in Jerusalem was destroyed amid the trumpet blasts of the conquering armies and a great measure of holiness departed from earth. At the new year the Jew looks forward to the restoration of the ancient glories.

(6) In the story of the binding of Isaac a ram was substituted for the lad. On *Rosh Ha-Shanah* we recall the merit of righteous ancestors by sounding the ram's horn and we are reminded that to give of the self in the service of God is of the essence of a true religious outlook on life.

(7) The prophet Amos asks: 'Shall the *Shophar* be blown in the city and the people be not afraid?' (*Amos* iii : 6) In ancient Palestine the *Shophar* was the sound of

alarm warning of the nearness of danger. We all know the harm that can be done by an excessive degree of fear in religion. But if our religion is not to be a sugary, sentimental thing it must remind us of the darker side of existence, that there are evils to be conquered both in the world outside and in the recesses of our own person- alities. And in authentic religious experience there is the sense of complete unworthiness in the presence of the Almighty. At least, this ingredient is there in all the accounts we have of those who have been subjected to such an experience. These feelings of seriousness, rever- ence and respect for life and for Him who gave it are awakened by the terrifying sound of the *Shophar*.

(8) The prophet Zephaniah speaks of the great 'day of the Lord', the Judgment Day, as a 'day of the *Shophar* and alarm'. (*Zeph.* i : 16) *Rosh Ha-Shanah*, the day of judgment, is a suitable time for reflection on the account we shall be called upon to give before the Throne of God for what we have made of our lives.

(9) The prophet Isaiah speaks of the great *Shophar* that will be sounded to herald the coming of the Messiah who will lead the scattered ones of Israel back to the land of their fathers (*Is.* xxvii : 13) and who will usher in a new era of peace for all mankind and the banishment of war from all the earth. Jews have never ceased to pray for the establishment of the Kingdom of Heaven on earth.

(10) The *Shophar* is to be sounded at the Resurrection. On the new year festival, when we pray for life, it is

well that we are reminded of the Jewish belief that the soul of man is immortal and that what he does with his life is of eternal significance.

Although the above reasons are given by Saadia most of them have their origin in earlier writings. The connection between the *Shophar* of *Rosh Ha-Shanah* and that of Sinai, for instance, is mentioned long before Saadia by Philo (20 B.C.E.). A second reason given by Philo is that the *Shophar* is a warlike instrument and is sounded on the festival as a grim reminder of the evils of war and to show the proper gratitude to God as the giver of peace.

Moses Maimonides (1135-1204), philosopher, teacher and codifier of Jewish law, the greatest Jew of the Middle Ages, writes, in the section of his Code which deals with Repentance:

> *Although it is a divine decree that we blow the* Shophar *on* Rosh Ha-Shanah *there is a hint of the following idea contained in the command. As if to say: 'Awake from your slumbers, ye who have fallen asleep in life, and reflect on your deeds. Remember your Creator. Be not of those who miss reality in the pursuit of shadows, and waste their years in seeking after vain things which do not profit or deliver. Look well to your souls, and let there be betterment in your acts. Forsake each of you your evil ways and thoughts.'*

The mystics have their own interpretation of the *Shophar*; they use the illustration of a lover serenading his beloved. Israel seeks to awaken the divine love and to link the higher and lower worlds. Others speak of the

Shophar sounds as a prayer without words. There is a longing in the human soul too deep to be conveyed in speech, which finds expression in the yearning notes of the *Shophar*. The *Shophar*, the wind instrument, is further said to symbolise the spiritual side of life (in Hebrew the word *ruah* means both 'wind' and 'spirit'). On *Rosh Ha-Shanah* man should be aware of the demands of the spirit in the year ahead and thus awaken the higher mercies.

Modern Jewish thinkers have given their interpretations of the *Shophar*. One of the finest of these is Milton Steinberg's exposition that the *Shophar* is a call to man to hear the sound of weeping humanity, to feel what the poet calls the *Weltschmerz*, the unspeakable pain of the world, and to resolve to do battle against all those forces working for man's oppression and subjugation, to the end that the day might come when the tear is wiped from every cheek and the sigh from every lip.

The Shophar Sounds

Rosh Ha-Shanah is described in Scripture as a 'day of blowing the horn' (*Num.* xxix : 1), *yom teruah* in Hebrew. The old Aramaic translation of *yom teruah* is *yom yebaba*, a day of *yebaba*. Of the mother of Sisera, who was defeated in the battle against the Israelites, it is said that she 'looked through the window *va-teyabeb*' (*Jud.* v : 28) which the Rabbis take to mean 'and she wept' (because her son had not returned from the battle). This is said to throw light on the meaning of *yom yebaba* as 'a day of

49

weeping' i.e. a day on which a weeping sound is made with the *Shophar*. But there is a tradition based on a careful examination of the relevant Biblical passages, that the *teruah*=*yebaba* must always be preceded by an extended note—the *tekiah*—and followed by the same note. As there are three references in Scripture to the *teruah* it is laid down that nine notes must be sounded on the *Shophar*, namely, *tekiah*, *yebaba*, *tekiah*, three times each. (As in so many other examples of Rabbinic exegesis the scriptural verses are not in themselves conclusive but it is clear that the Rabbis must have possessed certain basic traditions about such matters as the sounding of the *Shophar*. They must have been aware of the long-established custom and practice for *Rosh Ha-Shanah* although it is not always easy to discover whether a rule is based primarily on tradition or on Scriptural exegesis.)

In the course of time there arose doubts as to the precise nature of the 'weeping' sound. Did it mean a series of longer, groaning notes or did it mean short, sharp, wailing sounds? The series of longer notes (three in number) are called *shebharim* (from a root meaning 'to break'), the shorter, wailing notes (nine in number) are called *teruah*. In other words there is some uncertainty as to whether the *teruah*=*yebaba* of the Bible is the sound we now call *shebharim* or the sound we now call *teruah*, or, possibly, it is both of them combined. (In the act of weeping there are, at first, longer sighs and then short, staccato sobs.) Consequently, later Rabbis arranged that all three sets of sounds be made on the *Shophar*. If the letter *T* represents the sound *tekiah*, *S*, *shebharim*, and *Te*, *teruah*, the following is the set of sounds:

> TSTeT TSTeT TSTeT
> TST TST TST
> TTeT TTeT TTeT

The final *tekiah* of the whole set is extended and is known as *tekiah gedolah*, the great *tekiah*. In all congregations this set of thirty notes is sounded after the reading of the law. (R. 127, S. 165-166)

There are various customs with regard to the repetition of these sounds at other parts of the service. The custom of the United Synagogue of London is to sound *tekiah, shebharim, teruah, tekiah,* at the end of the three main divisions of the Reader's repetition of the additional service. (R. 157, 160 and 162, S. 210, 214 and 217) At the end of the service another thirty sounds are blown (the thirty sounds of the first set), generally before the *Adon Olam* hymn. (R. 171, S. 230) In many congregations further notes are sounded so as to total one hundred, said to correspond to the one hundred cries of the mother of Sisera. (Louis Ginzberg, the famed author of 'Legends of the Jews', suggested that the original reading here was not 'the mother of Sisera' but 'our mother Sarah' and the reference is to the tears shed by Sarah when she heard of Isaac's binding upon the altar. But, as we have seen, the Rabbis did connect the sounding of the *Shophar* with the weeping of Sisera's mother, though the precise significance of the number one hundred is far from clear. It is most remarkable that the theme of the 'weeping mother' occurs in many guises in the ritual of the new year festival.)

The three notes *tekiah, shebharim, teruah,* have received the attention of the symbolists. One view sees the three notes of weeping as different degrees of contrition, another view sees the *tekiah* as the optimistic note of confidence and hope that weeping will be turned to joy. Others interpret the three sounds as hesitation in approaching the King leading to increasing confidence as the suppliant is made welcome. Others again teach that the three notes correspond to three types of men. The firm, unwavering *tekiah* represents the good man, whose soul is undivided. The trembling *teruah* represents the wicked, full of remorse and regret, his soul torn in his unsuccessful struggle against evil. The *shebharim*, the partly broken notes, represent the average man, neither wholly good nor bad, who tries sincerely to make his life more complete.

The Laws of the Shophar

Originally the *Shophar* was sounded during the early morning service but it is said that in Roman times the *Shophar* sounds were sometimes mistaken for a summons to rebellion. The notes were sounded, consequently, during the additional service so that the lengthy prelude of prayer would convince the Roman authorities that the *Shophar* sounds were part of the festival ritual. The reason for sounding the *Shophar* both before and in the middle of the additional service is said to be in order to 'confuse Satan' when he attempts to bring Israel's sins before God. Whatever the original meaning of this curious idea it has been given this

interpretation. In Rabbinic literature Satan is iden-
tified frequently with the evil inclination in man. The
motif of 'confusing Satan' may, therefore, without undue
distortion, mean that by repeatedly sounding the *Shophar*
we are moved to control the darker forces in our nature.

Before the *Shophar* is sounded the special benediction
is recited: 'Who has sanctified us by Thy commandments
and commanded us to hear the sound of the *Shophar*'.
(R. 127, S. 165) Some earlier authorities favoured the
form: 'Who sanctified us ... and commanded us *to blow
the Shophar*'. The subtle, legal point involved is whether
the command is to *blow* the *Shophar* (the officiant who
blows in the Synagogue will then be said to blow on
behalf of the congregation) or to *hear* the *Shophar*. From
our form of the benediction it follows that we accept
the second opinion. This has enabled Jewish preachers to
exercise their homiletical skill in remarking that it is not
enough for man to sound the call to repentance with his
lips, he must hear it in his heart.

The Rabbis of the Talmud rule that one must hear
the actual sound of the *Shophar* and not its echo. Consequently, many present-day authorities are of the
opinion that the sounds of the *Shophar* must not be
relayed by loud-speaker, for this is analogous to hearing
the sound of the echo.

The congregation should stand while the *Shophar* is
sounded. In order to prevent mistakes occurring it is
customary for a member of the congregation to call out
each note before it is sounded. The *Shophar* should be
held facing towards the right with its mouth pointing

upwards. The *Shophar* must be blown at the narrow end so that the sound emerges from the wider end. In this connection the verse is quoted: 'Out of the *straits* I called upon the Lord; He answered me with great enlargement.' (*Ps.* cxviii : 5) To help us emerge from the narrow, restricted, egotistic view to the wider, more exalted one, to help us achieve a more magnanimous view of life and to emerge into a world of broader horizons, this is the purpose of all true religion.

The *Shophar* should be curved, not straight. The reason given for this is that the *Shophar* should be symbolic of man's willingness to bow in submission before the will of God.

According to the Rabbis, women are exempt from the performance of any positive precept which depends on time for its performance, that is, a precept that can only be carried out at a given time. (One of the reasons given is that it would be asking too much to expect women, with their many household cares and obligations, to lay aside their occupations in order to carry out this kind of religious duty.) However, although women are exempt from hearing the *Shophar*, it has long been the practice that they do come to the Synagogue to hear the *Shophar* being sounded. In Rabbinic terminology, this is one of those obligations which women, though exempt, have voluntarily assumed.

It is forbidden to blow the *Shophar* on the Sabbath. According to the Talmud this prohibition is of Rabbinic origin, the reason for it being that a person unfamiliar with the method of blowing may carry the *Shophar* into the public domain in order to consult an expert. It is consequently the rule that when the first day of *Rosh Ha-Shanah* falls on the Sabbath the *Shophar* is not sounded until the second day. The Jerusalem Talmud finds support for this rule in the different wording of the Biblical verses dealing with the *Shophar* on *Rosh Ha-Shanah*. In Leviticus (xxiii : 24) *Rosh Ha-Shanah* is described as 'a *memorial* proclaimed with the blast of horns', while in Numbers (xxix : 1) it is described as 'a day of *blowing* the horn'. The one verse is made to refer to the Sabbath when there is only a memory of the *Shophar* blasts, the other verse to the week-day when the *Shophar* is sounded. In the liturgy *Rosh Ha-Shanah* is called 'the day of blowing the horn' when it falls on a week-day, 'a day of memorial of the *Shophar*' when it falls on the Sabbath.

CHAPTER 6

LIFE AND ITS VALUES IN THE JEWISH TRADITION

Life

THE *Rosh Ha-Shanah* and *Yom Kippur* prayers vibrate with the theme of life. The Hebrew word for life, *hayyim*, occurs hundreds of times in the Festival Prayer Book. This is in accordance with Jewish teaching that life is God's precious gift to man and that the first precept of the *Torah* is 'be fruitful and multiply' (*Gen.* i : 28), the command that human life be perpetuated. From Biblical times 'length of days' has been among the most significant of Jewish blessings. Jewish tradition enjoins that we stand in the presence of 'the hoary head', the man rich in life's experience, whether, as the Rabbis teach, he is Jew or non-Jew. We have noted above the many instances in which the *Rosh Ha-Shanah* liturgy pays homage to the mother who brings life into the world. But Judaism would add that the supreme value of life is the opportunity it affords for serving God. 'Remember us unto life, O King, Who delightest in life, and inscribe us in the book of life, *for Thine own sake, O living God*'. The pupils of the great Gaon of Vilna were astonished when the famous scholar and saint wept on his deathbed. 'I believe with perfect faith', said the Gaon, 'in the life hereafter. But Heaven is the place where man is rewarded for his labours. It is here on earth that a man, for the price of a few copper coins, can perform deeds of inestimable worth.'

Saving Life

Judaism has always stressed the heinousness of the crime of taking life. Cain, the first murderer, is cursed by God and is condemned to wander over the face of the earth. While Judaism does not forbid a war of defence its attitude to war can be seen from the discussion in the *Mishnah* as to whether a man may go out on the Sabbath with a sword or bow or shield or club or spear. R. Eliezer permits it on the grounds that these are adornments. To which the sages reply: 'They are naught save a reproach, for it is written: "And they shall beat their swords into ploughshares, and their spears into pruning-hooks: nation shall not lift up sword against nation, neither shall they learn war any more." (*Is.* ii : 4)' Although David was described as 'a man after the Lord's heart' (*I Sam.* xiii : 14), he was not allowed to build the Temple because he was a warrior: '*Thou hast shed blood abundantly, and hast made great wars; thou shall not build a house unto my name.*' (*I Chron.* xxii : 8) In the life-affirming tradition of Judaism, the Rabbis remark that ten are called 'living'—God, the Torah, Israel, the righteous, Paradise, water, trees, the land of Israel, benevolence, and the wise.

In Jewish teaching the saving of life is among the highest of duties. Even the Sabbath may be profaned in order to save life. It is forbidden for man to endanger or to take any risks with his life. In the Rabbinic view, to neglect one's health is more serious than to offend against the religious law. Obviously, this regard for health must be extended to embrace the physical well-being of others. 'Regard for another's physical and material well-being is a spiritual concern', said a contemporary teacher. The verse: 'Neither shalt thou stand idly by the blood of thy neighbour' (*Lev.* xix : 16) was understood by the Rabbis as a warning against indifference to the fate of others.

Eternal Life and Life Here on Earth

Judaism teaches that the soul of man is immortal and his life eternal. The silence of Scripture (with the exception of very few passages) on the subject of the After-life cannot be attributed to unawareness on the part of the Scriptural writers, for the belief in immortality is deeply rooted in the consciousness of mankind and from the days of the Eygptian pyramids there was evidence of the part this belief played in religion. Indeed, the most plausible explanation of the comparative silence of Scripture on this matter is a conscious reaction to the death-oriented religion of peoples such as the Egyptians. Scripture appears to be saying that the God of Israel is the God of life here and now; and the task of man is the establishment of the Kingdom of Heaven on earth. 'That your days may be multiplied, and the days of your children, upon the land which the Lord swore unto your fathers to give them, *as the days of the heavens upon the earth.*' (*Deut.* xi : 21) The plain meaning of the concluding phrase of this verse is simply 'as long as the heavens endure'. But the homiletical interpretation, true to the spirit of Judaism, is that glimpses of heaven are to be obtained here on earth through the living of the good life—'*as the days of the heavens upon the earth*'. But Judaism, with all its emphasis on this world, is not indifferent to the wider hope. Post-Biblical Judaism teaches emphatically that life does not come to an end with the death of the body. Precisely because Judaism is a life-affirming religion it cannot allow us to believe that all man's yearning for abundant life is to be doomed to eternal frustration.

The truth of the matter is that in Judaism there exists the inevitable tension which stems from the teaching of this-worldly religion that life upon earth is a preparation for the After-life so that this life is 'a vale of soul-making'. This tension received its classic formulation in the striking paradox voiced by the second-century teacher, R. Jacob, who said: 'Better is one hour of repentance and good deeds in this world than the whole life of the world to come; yet better is one hour of blissfulness of spirit in the world to come than the whole life of this world!' The memorial prayers, recited on all the major festivals, are evidence of Judaism's other worldly approach; the omission of these prayers on *Rosh Ha-Shanah*, the feast of the beginning of the year, is evidence of Judaism's healthy this-worldliness.

The Quality of Life

Jewish teachers never tire of emphasising that it is not

the mere quantity of life which matters but its quality. Jewish tradition speaks of 'length of days and years' i.e. the ideal is a long life full of days well-spent in service. For the Rabbis a life, be it ever so long, without Torah, is an empty life, aimless, purposeless and totally inadequate. This idea was stated in dramatic fashion in the Rabbinic ruling that the man guilty of unintentional homicide, who, according to Biblical law, was obliged to fly to the city of refuge, could demand that his Torah teacher be exiled there with him. For, said the Rabbis, Scripture says that the guilty man should *live* in the refuge city and life without Torah is no life. Arising out of this emphasis on life's quality rather than its duration is the teaching that there are men whose lives, otherwise empty and devoid of value, can be utterly redeemed in a single act of moral greatness. Such men are spoken of as 'acquiring eternity in one moment of time'.

The name of Rab has been mentioned in these pages. Perhaps the finest summary of the unique Jewish philosophy of life, a remarkable blending of the spiritual and the material, is contained in a prayer, recited, we are told, by Rab each day and now read in the Synagogue on the Sabbath before the beginning of each new month: 'O grant us long life, a life of peace, of good, of blessing, of sustenance, of bodily vigour, a life marked by the fear of Heaven and the dread of sin, a life free from shame and reproach, a life of prosperity and honour, a life in which the love of the Torah and the fear of Heaven shall cleave to us, a life in which the desires of our heart shall be fulfilled for good.'

CHAPTER 7

THE JEWISH TEACHERS ON ROSH HA-SHANAH AND ITS THEMES: AN ANTHOLOGY

Some Extracts from the Talmud

(THE TALMUD is the gigantic work, enjoying in Jewish life an authority second only to the Bible. It was compiled towards the end of the fifth century of the present era, and contains the teachings of Jewish spiritual guides extending over a period of almost one thousand years. The Talmud has been translated into English under the editorship of Dr. I. Epstein.)

R. Abbahu said: Why do we blow on a ram's horn? The Holy One, blessed be He, said: Sound before Me a ram's horn so that I may remember on your behalf the binding of Isaac the son of Abraham and account it to you as if you had bound yourself before Me.

It is written: And it came to pass, when Moses held up his hand that Israel prevailed. (*Ex.* xvii : 11) Did the hands of Moses promote the battle or hinder the battle! It is, rather, to teach thee that such time as the Israelites directed their thoughts on high and kept their hearts in subjection to their Father in heaven, they prevailed; otherwise they suffered defeat. After the like manner thou mayest say: Make thee a fiery serpent and set it upon a standard, and it shall come to pass that everyone that is bitten when he seeth it he shall live. (*Num.* xxi : 8)

But could the serpent slay or the serpent keep alive! It is, rather, to teach thee that such time as the Israelites directed their thoughts on high and kept their hearts in subjection to their Father in heaven, they were healed; otherwise they pined away.

Hallel (*Ps.* cxiii-cxviii, recited in the Synagogue on the other festivals) is not said on *Rosh Ha-Shanah*. What is the reason? R. Abbahu replied: The ministering angels said in the presence of the Holy One, blessed be He: Sovereign of the Universe, why should Israel not chant hymns of praise before Thee on *Rosh Ha-Shanah* and the Day of Atonement? He replied to them: Is it possible that the King should be sitting on the throne of justice with the books of life and death open before Him, and Israel should chant hymns of praise?

Rabbah said: God proclaimed: Recite before Me on *Rosh Ha-Shanah* kingship, remembrance and *shophar* verses: kingship verses to declare Me king over you; remembrance verses, that the remembrance of you may come before Me for good; and through what? Through the *shophar*.

R. Eleazar said: A man should always first prepare himself for his prayer and then say it. R. Abba said: The diction of R. Eleazar appears to be well founded in respect of the blessings of *Rosh Ha-Shanah* and the Day of Atonement.

Iron breaks the stone, fire melts iron, water extinguishes fire, the clouds drink up the water, a storm drives away the clouds, man withstands the storm, fear unmans man, wine dispels fear, sleep drives away wine, and death sweeps all away—even sleep. But Solomon the Wise says: Charity saves from Death.

How can you escape sin? Think of three things: whence thou comest, whither thou goest, and to whom thou wilt have to account for all thy deeds: even to the King of Kings, the All Holy, praised be He.

If your God is a 'friend of the poor', asked a heathen of a Rabbi, why does He not support them? Their case, the sage answered, is left in our hands, that we may thereby acquire merits and forgiveness of sin. But what a merit it is! the other replied; suppose I am angry with one of my slaves, and forbid him food and drink, and someone goes and gives it him furtively, shall I be much pleased? Not so, the other replied. Suppose you are angry with your only son and imprison him without food, and some good man has pity on the child, and saves him from the pangs of hunger, would you be so very angry with the man? And we, if we are called servants of God, are also called his children.

Great is repentance, for it reaches to the Throne of Glory.
Great is repentance, for it lengthens the years of a man's life.
Great is repentance, for it makes the Redemption to come near.

The place which the penitent sinners occupy the perfectly righteous are unable to occupy.

The Holy One, blessed be He, said to Israel: My sons, open for Me an aperture of repentance as narrow as the eye of a needle, and I will open for you gates through which wagons and coaches can pass.

The gates of prayer are sometimes open and sometimes closed, but the gates of repentance are ever open. As the sea is always accessible, so is the hand of the Holy One, blessed be He, always open to receive penitents.

Whence is it derived that if one repents, it is imputed to him as if he had gone up to Jerusalem, built the Temple, erected an altar and offered upon it all the sacrifices enumerated in the Torah? From the verse: The sacrifices of God are a broken spirit. (*Ps.* li : 19)

One chastisement in the heart of man is better than many lashes.

Repentance and good deeds are man's advocates.

The following occurred to Benjamin the Righteous, who was in charge of the community charity chest. A woman came before him and said: Master take care of me.

By the Temple service! he said to her, there is nothing in the charity chest.

Master, she said to him, if thou dost not take care of me, thou wilt be the death of a widow and her seven sons. He thereupon gave her money from his own funds. Some time after, Benjamin the Righteous fell sick and lay in bed in pain. Said the ministering angels to the Holy One, blessed be He: Master of the Universe, Thou hast said: One who saves a single soul is as though he had saved the whole world. How much more so Benjamin the Righteous who saved a widow and her seven sons! Yet he is sorely sick.

Forthwith they beseeched mercy for him and his sentence was torn up. And twenty-two years were added to his life.

Maimonides on Prayer

(Moses Maimonides [1135-1204] is by general consent considered to be the most outstanding Jewish figure in the Middle Ages. The following is from M. Friedländer's translation of Maimonides' *Guide for the Perplexed*.)

We must bear in mind that all such religious acts as reading the Law, praying, and the performance of other precepts, serve exclusively as the means of causing us to occupy and fill our mind with the precepts of God, and free it from worldly business; for we are thus, as it were, in communication with God, and undisturbed by any other thing. If we, however, pray with the motion of our lips, and face toward the wall, but at the same time think of our business; if we read the Law with our tongue, whilst our heart is occupied with the building of our house, and we do not think of what we are reading; if we perform the commandments only with our limbs, we are like those who are engaged in digging in the ground, or hewing wood in the forest, without reflecting on the nature of those acts, or by whom they are commanded, or what is their object. We must not imagine that in this way we attain the highest perfection; on the contrary, we are then like those in reference to whom Scripture says, 'Thou art near in their mouth, and far from their reins'. (*Jer.* xii : 2)

I will now show you the way how to educate and train yourselves in order to attain that great perfection.

The first thing you must do is this: Turn your thoughts away from everything while you read *Shema* or during the *Tephillah*, and do not content yourself with being devout when you read the first verse of *Shema* or the first paragraph of the prayer. When you have successfully practised this for many years, try in reading the Law or listening to it, to have all your heart and all your thought occupied with understanding what you read or hear. After some time when you have mastered this, accustom yourself to have your mind free from all other thoughts when you read any portion of the other books of the prophets, or when you say any blessing; and to have your attention directed exclusively to the perception and the understanding of what you utter. When you have succeeded in properly performing these acts of divine service, and you have your thought, during their performance, entirely abstracted from worldly affairs, take then care that your thought be not disturbed by thinking of your wants or of superfluous things. In short, think of worldly matters when you eat, drink, bathe, talk with your wife and little children, or when you converse with other people. These times, which are frequent and long, I think, must suffice to you for reflecting on everything that is necessary as regards business, household, and health. But when you are engaged in the performance of religious duties, have your mind exclusively directed to what you are doing.

Maimonides on Charity

(These eight degrees of charity, based on earlier Rabbinic teaching, are recorded in Maimonides' great digest of Jewish Law—*Yad Ha-Hazakah*. The translation is that of Jacob M. Braude.)

The first and lowest degree of charity is to give, but

with reluctance or regret. This is the gift of the hand, but not of the heart.

The second is to give cheerfully, but not proportionally to the distress of the sufferer.

The third is, to give cheerfully, and proportionately, but not until solicited.

The fourth is, to give cheerfully, proportionately, and even unsolicited, but to put it in the poor man's hand, thereby exciting in him the painful emotion of shame.

The fifth is, to give charity in such a way that the distressed may receive the bounty, and know their benefactor, without their being known to him. Such was the conduct of some of our ancestors, who used to tie up money in the corners of their cloaks, so that the poor might take it unperceived.

The sixth, which rises still higher, is to know the objects of our bounty, but remain unknown to them. Such was the conduct of those of our ancestors who used to convey their charitable gifts into poor people's dwellings, taking care that their own persons and names should remain unknown.

The seventh is still more meritorious, namely to bestow charity in such a way that the benefactor may not know the relieved persons, nor they the names of their benefactors, as was done by our charitable forefathers during the existence of the Temple. For there was in that holy building a place called the Chamber of the Silent, wherein the good deposited secretly whatever their generous hearts suggested, and from which the poor were maintained with equal secrecy.

Lastly, the eighth, and the most meritorious of all, is to anticipate charity by preventing poverty: namely, to assist the reduced fellow man, either by a considerable gift, or a sum of money, or by teaching him a trade, or by putting him in the way of business, so that he may earn an honest livelihood, and not be forced to the dreadful alternative of holding out his hand for charity —this is the highest step of all.

A Penitential Prayer by Abraham Ibn Ezra

(Abraham Ibn Ezra [d. 1167] is famous in Jewish literature as a thinker, biblical exegete and poet. The translation is by Benzion Halper.)

I prostrate myself with my face to the ground, since nothing lower exists; I humbly cast myself down before the Most High, Who is the highest of all high.

O, wherewith shall I meet His countenance? If with my spirit, comes it not from Him? If with my choicest flesh? He gave it life, and man has naught that is nobler than his soul! There is no end and no beginning to His greatness—how can my tongue extol Him? Much farther is He than the heavens of the heavens, yet near to my flesh and bone.

Behold, I come to Thee, my God, because there is none besides Thee that can benefit. Have not all the hosts of heaven and of earth like me been created by Thy hand? How shall I then seek help from them? Is not the help of all created things in vain? A slave can flee to none for refuge, but unto his master who acquired him.

Why should I expect to know aught, knowing that

Thou hast created me for my good? Thy lovingkind-
nesses are more than can be told, but my sins exceed the
sand. How shall I lift up mine eye unto Thee, since mine
eye also has grievously transgressed? What more shall
my lips utter in response, since also they have dealt very
wickedly? The wantonness of my heart did unto me that
which my adversary could not do. Hot wrath has over-
taken me because of that; woe unto me, for I rebelled!
My evil inclination led me astray, for I desired not to
provoke Thee. My evils harmed only me, but Thou
alone wilt show me lovingkindness. Make known to me
a way to profit me, for Thou didst teach me all that I
know. I caused the prayers of my heart to be heard by
mine ears; mayest Thou hear them in heaven!

Joseph Albo's Interpretation of Malkhuyoth, Zikhronoth and Shopharoth

(Joseph Albo [d. about 1445] was a Spanish Jewish philosopher whose *Sepher Ha-Ikkarim*—The Book of Principles—is devoted to a discussion of the basic principles
of the Jewish faith. Albo reduces these principles to
three basic ideas—the existence of God, divine revelation, and reward and punishment. In the following
passage Albo expresses his conviction that these three
ideas are represented by the *Malkhuyoth*, *Zikhronoth* and
Shopharoth prayers. The translation is that of Isaac Husik.)

The blessing known as 'Kingdoms' corresponds to the
principle of the existence of God. This is proved by the
words of the benediction, 'Therefore do we wait for

Thee, O Lord our God, that we may quickly see Thy glorious strength, when the images will be removed from the earth and the idols will be completely cut off, when the world will be established under the Kingdom of the Almighty. . .when all the inhabitants of the world will recognise and know that to Thee shall every knee bend, by Thee every tongue swear. . .and all shall accept the yoke of Thy Kingdom.'

The benediction called 'Memorials' points to providence and reward and punishment, as is indicated by its contents: 'Thou rememberest the works of the universe, and visitest all the creatures from the beginning; before Thee are all hidden things revealed. . .'

The benediction called 'Trumpets' alludes to the third principle, revelation. Therefore it begins, 'Thou didst reveal Thyself in the cloud of Thy glory to Thy holy people and didst speak unto them. From heaven didst Thou cause them to hear Thy voice. . .'. This benediction is called Trumpets because at the time of the giving of the Law there was a very loud sound of the trumpet, such as never had been heard before in the world. Thunders and lightnings like those seen at Sinai or of the same nature had been heard and seen before, but the sound of a trumpet without a trumpet had never been heard before, and will not be heard again until the time of the redemption. At that time the true law will be made known before the whole world. This is the time that is referred to in the words of the prophet, 'And the Lord God will blow the horn' (*Zech.* ix : 14), according to some authorities.

Isaac Luria on Prayer

(Isaac Luria [1534-1572] one of the greatest of the Kabbalists wrote very little but his ideas were faithfully recorded by his disciple Hayyim Vital, from whose work the following is taken.)

It is forbidden to offer prayers to God in a melancholy spirit. One should pray as a servant who ministers to his Maker with great joy, otherwise the soul is powerless to receive the higher illumination which prayer draws down from above. It is only fitting for the worshipper to be sad when confessing his sins but during other parts of the service no sad thoughts should be present, even concern about the sins he has committed. Truly it is good for the worshipper to be in a humble frame of mind but a very joyful one. This is an exceedingly great principle of which it is proper to take note.

Samson Raphael Hirsch on Elul

(Samson Raphael Hirsch [1808-1888] was a powerful defender of Orthodoxy and leader of Jewish thought in Germany. The following is from Dr. I Grunfeld's translation of his essays.)

So the *shophar* of Elul penetrates into Jewish homes. Every Jewish breast awakes and looks around and above itself and before and after. It seeks the goal and examines the way and recognises the Lord and takes His will as a guide and measuring rod. It shakes itself out of its empty dream world. It strives to find its way back from the crooked path to the straight, from disobedience to faithfulness, from inattention to attention, and uses the few weeks which remain to it till the end of the year in order to impress on the spiritual work of the year the Jewish stamp of perfection.

Perfection? Does it dwell on earth? Is it ever attained? Is it attainable among men? Where is the man, where is the Jew, who could attain it or approach it? Take the purest, best, most faithful of men; how far he is from the uprightness which never swerves, from the obedience which never wavers, from the attention which never flags, such as is observed by every worm throughout its life! The purest, best, most faithful of men, how far is he from the goal, how weak in his loyalty, how shaky in his resolution! And if he should at last by a supreme effort recover the straight path and henceforth with serious and firm resolve preserve his loyalty, who will remove from the field of his future the seeds of mischief which have already been scattered there; who will uproot the germ of evil which the past already carries in its bosom; who will rescue him from the consequences of his own acts; who will draw him back from the grave which he has already dug for himself with every deviation, every display of unfaithfulness and inattention?

Observe how alongside of the solemn call of the *shophar* the gentle voice of the Divine teaching speaks to you and says: 'The same God Who created the strict law of premiss and consequence, of cause and effect, Who enclosed within the confines of this law every other thing that exists from the worm to the eagle, from the grain of dust to the orb of the sun, Who with His power guides every other thing that exists along the track of this law and keeps it in the path of this law without deviation—this same God has created you as the free minister of His will.' And since He made you free and with this freedom gave to you alone the capability of crookedness, of disobedience, of negligence, therefore, when He created you He combined love with His justice and grace with His might. He infused into the spark of freedom with which He inspired you a breath of His power, and promised it victory in a ceaseless struggle against the forces of blind necessity to which everything else is subject. Only crookedness, disobedience, negligence, the man who divests himself of his freedom, succumbs to the pressure of that iron law. But when a man reasserts his freedom and returns to his allegiance, then God takes note of his tear of repentance, of his sincere resolve, and crushes before them the evil seed of his heart. The curse-laden germ which the past has already imbibed perishes in their presence. The pure tear is stronger, the pure will conquers the law which holds heaven and earth in its spell; the grace of God makes the free man free.

Franz Rosenzweig on Rosh Ha-Shanah

(Franz Rosenzweig's [1886-1929] 'Star of Redemption', from which the following extract is taken, is one of the greatest attempts to interpret Judaism for the modern age. The translation is by Nahum N. Glatzer.)

The horn blown on New Year's Day at the peak of the festival stamps the day as a 'day of judgment'. The judgment usually thought of as the end of time is here placed in the immediate present. And so it cannot be the world that is being judged—for where could the world be at this very present? It is the individual who faces judgment. Every individual is meted out to his destiny according to his actions. The verdict for the past and coming year is written on New Year's Day, and it is sealed on the Day of Atonement, when the last reprieve constituted by these ten days of penitence and turning to God is over. The year becomes representative of eternity, in complete representation. In the annual return of this day of judgment, eternity is stripped of every trace of the beyond, of every vestige of remoteness; it is actually there, within the grasp of every individual and holding every individual in its strong grasp. He is no longer part of the eternal history of the eternal people, nor is he part of the eternally changing history of the world. There is no more waiting, no more hiding behind history. The individual confronts judgment without any inter-mediary factor. He stands in the congregation. He says 'We'. But the 'We' of this day are not the 'We' of the people in history; the sin for which we crave forgiveness is not the sin of transgression of laws which separates this people from the other peoples of the world. On these days the individual in all his naked individuality stands before God.